INTELLECT TO INCOME

Intellect to Income– The Ultimate Playbook
How to Turn Your Degrees, Education and Experience into a Lucrative Lifestyle Business

First Edition

First published in the USA in 2023

Paperback ISBN: 978-1-958405-83-3
eBook ISBN: 978-1-958405-84-0
Hardcover ISBN: 978-1-958405-86-4
Library of Congress Control Number: 2023911960

Spotlight Publishing House™ in Goodyear, AZ
https://spotlightpublishinghouse.com

Editors: Cori Wamsley and Renee Picard
Book Cover: Angie Ayala
Interior Design: Marigold2k

Shevelle McPherson, ESQ

INTELLECT TO INCOME

The Ultimate Profit Playbook

How to Turn Your Degrees, Education and Experience into a Lucrative Lifestyle Business

SHEVELLE MCPHERSON, ESQ.

SPOTLIGHT
PUBLISHING HOUSE

Goodyear, Arizona

LEGAL AND FINANCIAL DISCLAIMER

The material in this book is for informational purposes only. It is not to be construed as legal advice or a substitute for seeking legal advice from a licensed attorney. The sole purpose is to provide information and education, not to create an attorney-client relationship. Although the author is an attorney, she is not the reader's attorney. This book does not create an attorney-client relationship between the reader and McPherson Law or Shevelle McPherson. The reader is encouraged to consult with a licensed attorney in their state regarding their specific legal questions and concerns.

Although the publisher, author, and editor have made every effort to ensure that the information in this book was correct at press time and while this publication is designed to provide accurate information in regard to the subject matter covered, the publisher and the author assumes no responsibility for errors, inaccuracies, omissions, or any other inconsistencies herein and hereby disclaim any liability to any party for any loss, damage, or disruption caused by errors or omissions, whether such errors or omissions result from negligence, accident, or any other cause.

The publisher, author, and editor make no guarantees concerning the level of success you may experience by following the advice and strategies contained in this book, and you accept the risk that results will differ for each individual.

Praise for Intellect to Income

When I came to Shevelle, I was a business owner who was literally all over the place. I was making money, but I was not confident in how to grow my business. After working with Shevelle in her Intellect to Income program and putting her profit pillar system in place, I increased my revenue from five figures to multiple six figures. Thank you, Shevelle!

—Margo Masri, CFO
Founder, Masri Accounting Solutions

In just over four months of working with Shevelle in her Intellect to Income program and putting her profit pillar system in place, I significantly increased my revenue. This system works!

—Jonathan Bengel, Enrolled Tax Agent
Author, Speaker, Coach, and Founder of JB Financial

Wow! I got my first client in four weeks working with Shevelle! I've been through other programs, but Intellect to Income is the most comprehensive and the simplest. Plus, it works! Thank you, Shevelle.

—Haseena Patel, Author, Coach and Speaker
Founder of Truth Walker - South Africa

Dedication

To all those with degrees, education, talent, and expertise who are ready to share your knowledge with the world on a much grander scale, this book is dedicated to YOU. As an author, I get inspired by my fellow experts, business owners, and degree holders eager to take their intellect to the next level. I am passionate about supporting you in leveraging and monetizing your intellect so you can finally experience ultimate time, financial, and location freedom.

Because you are reading this book, it is evident that you have taken the first step toward achieving this goal. My aim is to equip you with the tools you need to identify, package, and monetize your intellect in a leveraged way. After reading this book, you will be able to move beyond being a commodity, transition from that stressful career, stop trading time for money, and escape the entrepreneurial profit hamster wheel. By doing so, you can increase your earning potential without compromising profit, time, or lifestyle.

It's time to go from being stuck and stagnant to freedom and flexibility. The moment to monetize YOU has arrived!

Shevelle

Acknowledgments

Special thank you to my parents, bonus parents, siblings, son, as well as my close friends and family who support me in all my endeavors. Your steadfast belief in me is greatly appreciated. I shall be forever grateful. I love each and every one of you to infinity and beyond!

Contents

Preface

Who this book is for:

Intellect to Income: The Ultimate Profit Playbook is a roadmap for professionals (attorneys, accountants, therapists, coaches and other professional service providers) and entrepreneurs who want to transform their education and experience into a lucrative lifestyle business. As a business growth strategist and international speaker, I have met and worked with numerous professionals and entrepreneurs who work tirelessly yet struggle to maintain consistent cash flow.

After working with many of you, I've found that the two most common struggles you encounter are:

1. Not knowing how to strategically monetize your intellect, and
2. Not having a proven profit system.

Many professionals and entrepreneurs have exceptional qualifications in the form of degrees, education, experience, certifications, training, and/or skills but do not know how to turn their knowledge and talent into consistent profit doing what they love. This situation can leave you feeling trapped in soul-sucking jobs, burning out in stressful careers, or running businesses that consume all your time without producing adequate profit.

If you can relate, you've probably already said this to yourself more than once: *Something's got to change.*

Intellect to Income: The Ultimate Profit Playbook is your gateway to change. It is designed to help you break free from this cycle. In this playbook, I share my proven 5 Pillar Profit System, which outlines the step-by-step process of building a profit machine around your intellect.

You see, I understand what it feels like to be stuck, burned out, and stagnant. I have been there before, trading my time for money and working long hours in a career I began to despise. Even after leaving that career to start my own "dream" business, I found myself working even longer hours trying to grow the business, which consumed me, leaving me with very little time to enjoy life.

I was on the road to burn out. Until, one day, the life of the "grind" came to a screeching halt. This was my first aha moment.

I had a speaking engagement where I spoke to a group of entrepreneurs. I had the opportunity to sell my intellect, which was packaged in the form of a digital course, at the end of my talk. I had many previous speaking engagements, but this was the first one that permitted me to make a paid offer at the end.

I recall that moment vividly: I made more in that one hour than I had in a year at my previous job.

This was a huge revelation, and it's where I discovered my pathway to profit, time, and lifestyle freedom.

I began traveling the world, living a "work from wherever" life, where I continued speaking and selling my packaged intellect in the form of either a digital course or group coaching program. This led to a lucrative freedom lifestyle.

My success inspired me to teach my private clients my 5 Pillar Profit System so they could experience the time, location, and financial freedom that I was enjoying. Moreover, they could do what they love like I was (and am!).

Now I am sharing this system with you in this profit playbook so you can monetize your intellect, leave the soul-sucking job behind, stop trading time for money, move beyond 1:1 client work, or transition out of that stressful career so you can gain time, financial, and location freedom too.

Are you ready to leverage and monetize your intellect, turn it into a profit machine, and have greater impact, influence, and income while living a life you absolutely love?

Let's do this!

The First Play

"Do Not SCIIP" the Legal Side"

Profit Pillar #1 – Legalize

A Rock-Solid Legal Foundation

"I'm embarrassed to say this, but I have nothing in place"
...the legal foundation dilemma.

I was on stage speaking live to about 300 entrepreneurs at a business conference talking about the importance of getting "Legally Bossed Up," meaning to have a legal foundation in place in your business. My talk laid out my 5 Legal Pillars, the legal foundation every business should have. I kept my pulse on the audience as I did a visual scan of the room during my talk, as I always do when speaking. Talking about "legal stuff" is not very exciting for most entrepreneurs, although it's THE MOST IMPORTANT aspect of any business, so I try to keep it upbeat and entertaining. The audience seemed very engaged and was soaking it all in. Some were taking copious notes, others were nodding in agreement at various points in my talk, and many appeared to have their eyes glued to me on stage, tuned in to my every word as though they were trying to process all the jewels I kept dropping. It was apparent that my talk was resonating with the audience.

One woman in particular really caught my attention. At various points in my speech, she did all the things I just described. She seemed super engaged. At the end of my talk, I invited everyone in the audience to stop by my speaker booth if they had any additional questions. The woman who caught my eye (the super-engaged one) was the first to get up. She bolted to the back of the room as though her winning numbers were just announced at Bingo. I ended my talk and headed to the back of the room to find a long line of entrepreneurs waiting to speak to me. The super-engaged woman, whom I later learned was named Devorah, was first in line. I greeted Devorah and then asked her my infamous "after my speech" question: "So, what part of my talk resonated with you the most and led you to meet me at the back of the room?" Devorah responded: "OMG! All of it."

I was not surprised because most entrepreneurs "SCIIP" (structure, contracts, intellectual property, insurance, procedures) putting all the legal pillars I laid out in my talk in place. I responded: "Ok, so how can I help you." Devorah responded: "Can you help me put all my legal pillars in place? I'm a psychotherapist, and I've been in business for 23 years. I'm embarrassed to say this, but I never thought to put any legal pillars in place. Now I've launched a new business, and I don't want to put that business at risk. I have nothing in place. After hearing your talk, I know *what* I need in place, but I do not know *how* to do it."

I responded: "No reason to be embarrassed. You are not alone. You see the long line behind you? I bet most of those entrepreneurs haven't put all of their legal pillars in place either—and, just like you, probably don't know how. What matters is you now know you need a solid legal foundation. You understand how important it is, and you are ready to take action to put it in place. So, when would you like to get started putting it all in place?" She responded: "Yesterday!" I chuckled and then gave her an appointment to speak to me privately. (There are several ways I work with clients, and I needed to assess her specific situation to determine how to best serve her.)

Most entrepreneurs build their businesses just like Devorah. They get so excited about their business idea and making money that they totally ignore the most important part of their business, the legal side. I know because I get the "uh oh" phone calls, 911 text messages, and frantic emails all the time. This doesn't usually end well and is NEVER wise.

Having a solid legal foundation is imperative to you not only making money but keeping it. Think about it: would you move into a house with no foundation? Probably not. But for whatever reason many entrepreneurs think it is okay to build and move into a business with no legal foundation.

Hopefully, you've read *Legally Bossed Up: The Ultimate Legal Playbook*, the first part of this four-part book sequel, because it covers this play in depth and shares real life stories that show why ignoring the legal side of your business is never a good idea. If you've read the book and implemented your legal plays you can head straight on over to play number two, where we begin to focus on the profit side of your business. If you haven't read that book (which I suggest you do), this First Play will give you an overview of the five essential legal pillars that are the foundational pillars of your business and that you should never SCIIP. Before you set out to become profitable, you MUST ensure you have laid a legal foundation to support and KEEP you profiting in your business, without interruption.

The best time to put your legal foundation in place is at the onset of starting your business. If you haven't done that, no worries… the next best time is NOW!

So, let's dive in.

The 5 Legal Pillars

I. Structure - **Your Property Shield**

> Every business needs a house (shelter). I call this having a Protective Legal Structure (PLS) to personally shield you from the liabilities incurred by your business.

There are four primary types of business structures and the C.O.L.T.ure (complexity, ownership, liability, and taxation) of each are different.[1] In addition, only two of the four business structures are PLSs that provide limited liability protection.

Types of Business Structures and their C.O.L.T.ure

1. **Sole Proprietorship (SP)** – A for-profit enterprise that is owned and operated by one person. It is not a PLS.

---

[1] These business structures are based on U.S. business entity principles. If you are trying to select a business structure outside of the United States, the information in this chapter will not likely apply to you. However, most countries have similar business structures. I highly recommend reading this chapter for a general understanding of how to select the proper entity and then researching and comparing the various structures in the country where you are seeking to register your business. I recommend seeking the advice of a licensed legal practitioner in your country regarding your specific needs.

2. **Partnership** – A for-profit enterprise that is owned by two or more persons. There are two types of partnerships: The General Partnership (GP) and the Limited Liability Partnership (LLP)
   a. **General Partnership (GP)**:
   Owned by two or more individuals who all have unlimited liability for the debts and liabilities of the business. It is not a PLS.

   b. **Limited Liability Partnership** (**LLP**) – Owned by two or more individuals. At least one owner must be a GP who is responsible for the day-to-day business operations, and at least one owner must be an LP, not involved in the day-to-day business operations. The GP has no limited liability whereas the LP does. The LLP is a PLS for the LP but not for the GP.

3. **Limited Liability Company (LLC)** – A business form that allows owners, who are referred to as "members," to enjoy limited liability while avoiding the complex operation and taxation of a corporation. It is a separate legal entity and a PLS.

4. **Corporation**
   a. **C-Corp** – A for-profit entity, a separate legal entity, and a PLS that is owned by shareholders and managed by a board of directors. The board must appoint officers (such as a CEO, president, treasurer, and secretary) to supervise daily corporate business.

   b. **S-Corp** – An S Corp is a tax classification rather than a standalone legal structure. An S-Corp is typically an LLC or C-Corp that qualifies for special tax treatment under the Internal Revenue Code and State Corporate Statutes.

It is generally wise to select a PLS as a business structure, so your liability is limited. This means that you shield yourself from any liability incurred by your business. The LLP (for the limited partner only), LLC, C-Corp, and S-Corp are PLSs. If you need more clarity around determining which PLS is best for you, scan the QR code at the end of this play to get access to a free bonus, my business structure comparison chart.

II. Contracts - Your Profit Shield

A contract is a legally enforceable agreement between two or more competent adults each promising to act (or refrain from acting) in exchange for some form of consideration (usually money or a benefit). For example, an agreement to perform a service in exchange for monetary compensation.

Contracts set boundaries at the onset of business relationships and can help prevent or resolve future disputes, so they are essential to have.

You should use effective legal agreements with all those you engage in business with.

III. Intellectual Property Protection - Your IP Shield

Everything related to your content and branding is your intellectual property (IP). Entrepreneurs and creatives typically spend a lot of time creating content, such as for programs and blogs, which need to be protected as IP. Other examples of IP include branding assets like logos, taglines, designs, and other items that identify your products and services as unique. Even if you aren't selling something, your brand can incur damage when infringers (copycats) steal your original creative work, your brand likeness, and/or your content in an unauthorized manner. The best way to protect your IP from improper use, exploitation, and outright theft is through copyright and trademark protection.

Copyright law protects original literary works that an author/creator has created by their own intellectual effort. This includes written work, musical and dramatic work, artistic work, and software.

Trademark law protects your brand. A trademark is a mark that identifies a service, product, business, or brand. Your trademark serves as an identifier of a source of services or goods. This helps prevent brand confusion in the marketplace. Trademark protection covers words, distinguishing marks, logos, taglines, and phrases, designs and symbols, business names, and product labels.

Three key benefits of registering your copyright with the United States Copyright Office and your trademark with the United States Trademark Office (The Three Ps):

1. **Proof of Ownership** – You get a registration certificate evidencing you as the owner of the registered IP.
2. **Protection** – Copyright and trademark registration guarantees protection from the federal government.
3. **Penalties** – Hefty penalties can be imposed on IP infringers when you register your intellectual property with the federal government, including attorney fees.

IV. Insurance - Your Risk Shield

Every business owner wants to be profitable and build wealth. This means putting measures in place to reduce risks and liability. The problem is that operating any business exposes you to risk. It's extremely important to have proper business insurance in place when you first start your business — I suggest getting it right when you finish reading this play if you have not yet done so. This will reduce those unanticipated inherent risks.

Insurance is about shifting unanticipated risk to a third party — an insurance company. One lawsuit or catastrophic event could be enough to completely wipe out your small business before it gets a chance to soar and create long-term wealth. That's why business insurance can be critically important to the survival of your business.

V. Processes - Standard Operating Procedures and Automation Systems

1. Standard Operating Procedures

What are Standard Operating Procedures (SOPs)?
SOPs help businesses run efficiently and effectively. Simply put, they are clear step-by-step task instructions. SOPs eliminate confusion, ambiguity, and inconsistency regarding legal landmines you want to avoid. SOPs also foster increased productivity, eliminate wasted time, and reduce workplace injuries.

Creating an SOP manual with all your SOPs can not only help your business remain compliant with regulations and improve employee training but also provide a consistent step-by-step guide for completing essential business tasks in your business. Having this type of roadmap is vital, especially if you or another key person needs to step away from the business for a period of time.

You should identify the procedures or tasks in your business that can be standardized—for instance, new client onboarding—and develop step-by-step directions for completing that task. These instructions can become the SOP for this task and should be added to your SOP manual. I recommend doing this for every task that is important in keeping your business running smoothly.

2. **Automation Systems**

What is Automation?

Automation is software that allows businesses to enhance productivity and improve customer service and retention (which ultimately increases the profitability of the business) while minimizing mistakes in processes and procedures. This reduces the risk of errors and litigation. Simply put, automation is putting specific tasks on autopilot so your business can run smoothly and efficiently, protecting your client relationships and profit.

Some business tasks are so mundane and routine that they are worth automating rather than hiring staff members to perform. These routine business tasks can typically be completed by using the automation of CRM, a customer relationship management tool.

What is a CRM?

A CRM is software that allows a company to optimize and organize its customer relations and can be critical to the sustainability of your business. Every business should have a robust CRM to manage client relationships.

Devorah hired me and joined my program. As a result, she implemented the first play. She put all her legal pillars in place. Here's what she had to say:

"Thanks to Shevelle McPherson, Esq., and her wisdom and knowledge as a legal and business growth strategist, I realized that my holistic therapy business, which I've had for 23 years, had been run more like a metaphorical 'lemonade stand' than an actual adult business.

Nothing was official: no LLC, no EIN, no contracts, and no separate business bank account. All that has changed since working in Shevelle's Intellect to Income Program. Not only did I get my legal biz in order, but I also went from charging $125 an hour in my new coaching business to selling $7,500 premium high-ticket coaching packages in 90 days. I now have new boundaries and clarity in my business. As a result, I am better serving my clients and have had huge successes both personally and financially. Feeling grateful and excited about the future of my business.

Thanks, Shevelle!"

Now it's time for you to get your legal biz in order!

Let's Make the First Play

Now that you know the 5 Legal Pillars you need to implement for a proper legal foundation, let's put Profit Pillar #1 – Legalize in place:

Don't SCIIP this play! Implement it now and get your legal foundation in place.

Implement The First Play, and then complete the checklist:

I. **S**tructure – Select a PLS, putting your Property Shield (PLS) in place: ____________________

II. **C**ontracts – Get effective legal agreements, putting your Profit Shield in place________________
(You can go to www.myprofitprotector.com to get effective legal agreement templates.)

III. **I**P – Trademark and copyright your IP, putting your IP Shield in place________________________

IV. **I**nsurance – Get appropriate business insurance, putting your Risk Shield in place ____________

V. **P**rocedures and Processes– Create your SOPs and get a robust CRM, putting your systems shield in place.
(Keap is a robust CRM that I use.

Go to www.legallybossedup.com/keapfreetrial to get a 14-day trial if you don't already have a CRM.)

If you've completed the checklist…

Congratulations!

You have set up the legal foundation in your business and **Pillar #1 - Legalize** is in place.

Listen to my personal message and download a free copy of my Business Structure Comparison Chart by scanning the code below or go to:

https://www.intellecttoincome.com/bizchart

The Second Play

The Attractive EPPIC Expert Character

Profit Pillar #2 – Attraction

"That will be $50,000 for my services."
...the attractive EPPIC expert effect

The Road from Commodity to Attractive EPPIC expert...

The Commodity Journey

"Finish school. You need to get a good education so you can get a good job." This was all I heard growing up. I heard it from my parents, grandparents, and even my high school guidance counselor while encouraging and helping me apply for college. Like many others, it was ingrained in my head to become a commodity at an early age, although I didn't realize that at the time. So, I did as I was advised. I finished high school, graduated college, completed paralegal school, and started my legal career working for a law firm as a paralegal.

As a paralegal, I worked 40 hours a week in exchange for a $28,000 annual salary. While working this paralegal job, I decided to go to law school. My thought was: *if I can just get more education and become a lawyer, I can earn more money.* (The commodity mindset was a big factor in this decision.) So, after obtaining a dual bachelor's degree, a paralegal certificate, and working as a paralegal for a few years, I went to law school and received my juris doctorate degree.

After graduating from law school with my juris doctorate degree, I started my attorney career as a prosecutor, an assistant district attorney (ADA) for the City of Philadelphia. While working as an ADA, I also obtained my master's degree in trial advocacy.

My ADA journey was rewarding and demanding at the same time. I would wake up early and go to bed late. As a municipal court prosecutor (my initial assignment), I was responsible for handling about 50 criminal cases a day. At that time, municipal court cases were handled in the district courts, so I would wake up around 6:00 am and drive to my assigned district court, lugging about 50 criminal case files in my rolling litigation bag.

Once I arrived, I sat at the prosecutor's table in the courtroom, unloaded all my case files, and then began to speak to the police officers, witnesses and adversary attorneys about the respective cases. Once this preliminary hearing preparation was done, the judge would enter the courtroom, and the daily court session would begin. I would then stand at the bar of the court from 8:00 am on, calling witness after witness as I prosecuted one case at a time, until all my cases were addressed. This usually took up most of the morning and part of the afternoon, on a good day.

Afterward, I would pack my rolling litigation bag, head back to my car, and drive to the office of the district attorney (DA) in Center City where I would then sit in my cubicle in a room full of cubicles occupied by other prosecutor attorneys who were also prepping cases. I would spend a few hours marking up the case files that I had litigated that day, and then I would begin to prepare the 50 new cases waiting on my desk for the next day. Somewhere in between I would grab a bite to eat. It would usually be late in the evening when my daily ADA tasks were complete. I would then head home to retire for the evening, sometimes bringing work home to finish prepping if it got too late and I didn't want to stay at the DA's office late in the night completing my case prep work. This was my daily routine for the first two years serving as an ADA.

After two years I was promoted to the Juvenile Unit, and after a few months there I was promoted to the Major Trial Unit. Once in the major trial unit, I was assigned to a trial team in Common Pleas Court. Common Pleas Court cases started at 9:00 am and were handled at the Criminal Justice Center (CJC) in Center City Philadelphia, walking distance from the DA's office so I could wake up a little later now, since I no longer had to be in court at 8:00 am or travel to the district court.

The workload didn't decrease much, but the assigned cases required more attention and strategy, as they were major crime cases at the jury trial stage. My daily routine now consisted of driving into Center City, heading into the DA's office, grabbing my files and rolling litigation bag, and then walking to the CJC to handle my daily case load. Afterwards, I would walk back to the DA's office and perform the same routine, marking up the files I resolved for the day before preparing for the next day's heavy case load and /or trial. I did this for almost two years. After spending a total of about four years in the DA's office, I decided to venture out into private practice and start my own law firm.

The Awakening of the "Attractive EPPIC Expert"

When I left the DA's office, I was making $48,000 per year. Although I didn't make a lot of money as an ADA, I gained a TON of experience. In fact, that experience, coupled with the master's degree in trial advocacy I had obtained, made me a very attractive criminal litigation expert when I transitioned into private practice and began operating my own law firm. I began handling business and criminal cases: the practice areas most aligned with my background, training, education, and experience.

Criminal clients were attracted to me like I was a magnet. Once they learned I was a former prosecutor with criminal trial training and experience, word began to spread through the jails like wildfire. Not to mention I began to "beat" (win) a lot of my criminal cases. I started to develop an expert reputation as one of the "go-to criminal defense lawyers," and I became sought after.

I recall one of my first serious criminal cases, a murder. The defendant's family met with me for a legal consultation in my office to discuss the facts of the case and possible defenses. Then they asked the usual question: "How much will it cost to retain your services?" I responded, "Homicide retainers start at $30,000, and because he has other open matters, it will be $50,000 to get started." Without hesitation they replied, "Not a problem. How can we pay you?" They hired me.

At that point in my career, I signed on "one" case for a little more than the amount I had earned in "one year" as a former ADA working for the City of Philadelphia. This was my first aha moment, it was the awakening of the attractive EPPIC expert. I realized that I had acquired valuable intellect. All the degrees, education, and experience I had acquired, coupled with the experience I had gained working several years as an ADA, was VALUABLE. It allowed me to go from almost $50,000 a *year* working for the government to $50,000 a *case* in private practice (the marketplace). I call this the attractive EPPIC expert effect.

Step into Your Attractive EPPIC Expert Character

Every great business must have an attractive EPPIC expert, and YOUR business is no different. Your vast amount of experience, coupled with your degrees, formal education, and/or training is valuable and can position you as an EPPIC attractive expert in the marketplace. To create a profitable lifestyle business, you must first step into your attractive EPPIC expert character.

The Second Play is all about becoming EPPIC. Identifying your:

I. **E**xpertise
II. **P**erfect Dream Client (PDC)
III. **P**ressing Problem that you Solve – it must be urgent (UPS)
IV. **I**nstant Attraction – your Magnetizing Marketing Message (MMM)
V. **C**larity – Creative Envision Board (CEB)

I. EXPERTISE

In a job and or career, you are treated as a commodity, not an expert. You are hired and get paid a fixed amount of money to fill a position and perform specific job tasks, per the job description. At some point, most of us were (some of us still are) treated as a commodity. As a commodity, you typically work for a company, organization, or institution and you are paid to perform the "job" for which you were hired. After all, most of us were groomed to do exactly this: complete school and get a good job in the workplace—a company, institution, or government. What we were *not* told is that our intellect is actually much more valuable in the marketplace as opposed to the workplace.

When I was hired for $50,000 for one of my first murder cases in private criminal law practice (this was around what I earned working for an entire year as a prosecutor), it was the result of first being seen as an expert in the context of the marketplace. I was referred to my client by someone I successfully resolved a serious case for, and my client knew I was a former major crimes prosecutor with litigation skills and experience. I was the attractive expert character in my business. I had a unique skill set and intellect, and these were highly valued by those needing a high level of expertise in criminal litigation.

Although I had previously received a mere $48,000 for a year's worth of hard work, it is that work, nearly four years of on-the-job training as a prosecutor, coupled with my degrees, education, and perspective, that allowed me to develop mastery. That mastery—my intellect—is much more valuable in the legal marketplace than it was in the government.

Some people elect to remain in a commodity type of position for their own reasons and that is OK. In fact, starting in such a role enhances your skillset and prepares you for the marketplace. Others, however, get the "entrepreneurial bug" and decide to venture off into the marketplace. If you are going to take that leap and you want to maximize your profitability, you must be seen as an expert.

As an expert in the marketplace, you are viewed as a unique problem solver, not a commodity. People will pay you money in exchange for your unique way of solving their problem(s). You are not just "filling a position." You are seen as a culmination of your training, education, background, experience, and unique perspective. And once you become known as an expert in solving a *big* problem, the marketplace will pay you a *premium price* for your unique expert solution. My criminal client had a big problem—he was facing life in prison—so $50,000 to try to regain his freedom and reputation was a no-brainer price. He knew to seek out an expert, someone who specialized or had vast experience in criminal litigation.

Just imagine if you need heart surgery, you will likely seek out a cardiologist, a doctor that specializes in caring for the heart rather than a general practitioner. Why is that? We all know that repetition breeds mastery. The cardiologist repeatedly works with the heart, in fact, that's all he works on, so his skill set in this particular area is focused and specialized. The cardiologist is an expert, highly sought after, and is paid a premium price for his services.

This is exactly how you must be in your business. If you master your craft and put yourself out there as the "cardiologist" of your area of expertise, you can monetize your expert skillset. Mastery leads to money.

To monetize your degrees, education, and experience, you must first identify YOUR area of expertise, your special skill(s), and your knowledge. Remember, experts typically specialize in one specific area and get paid way more than generalists who perform several types of services. This is because experts have mastery and are sought after. They are like celebrities; people gravitate toward them. They are naturally attractive.

So, the first step in turning your intellect into income is to determine your area of expertise, the area you have mastery in, and prepare to put it in the marketplace. You may be "good" at many things, but it's time to identify the ONE thing you will focus on. You don't have to be a lawyer or cardiologist to be an expert. You simply must have more knowledge, skill, or experience than those in the market you plan to help.

As I was once told, "A fourth grader is a third grader's hero."

Determining your ONE area of expertise to monetize

When determining your expertise, you can look at several factors. Look at the areas you have degrees, training, experience, knowledge, certificates, or challenges in your own life that you have overcome. I call these your Intellect to Income (ITI) Expert Factors.

Let's examine your ITI Expert factors: Answer the following questions.

- What are you good at?
- What topic do you have degrees, certificates, education, experience, skills, training, or licenses in?
- What do people constantly ask to pick your brain about?
- What have you helped others with in the past?
- What problems have you solved for yourself in the past?
- What are you naturally good at doing?
- If asked to speak, what topic could you speak on with no preparation?
- What do you love to do and would do for free if you could?

Answering those ITI expert factor questions can help reveal your area of expertise. You must identify it. If you don't have formal education or training but you've figured out a solution to a big problem you were struggling with or that you've helped someone else with, you may have an expert solution that the market is willing to pay for (e.g., weight loss, marketing, healthy eating, etc.) As long as you have more mastery than the person or market you are helping, and you can solve their biggest problem, you likely have monetizable intellect.

Start by getting really clear on your area of expertise. Getting clear will allow you to hone in on your "genius zone," and help you understand who will pay the most for your solution. It will also allow you to steer away from shiny bright objects and opportunities that don't truly serve you because they are outside your zone of expertise. I recommend you pick a lane and own it. Be the Saks Fifth Avenue or Walmart of your industry. Pick one area and monetize it. You may be gifted at many things, but you must start by choosing ONE area to focus on.

Once you have built a solid business around that, you can embark on new ventures, but the initial goal is to focus on ONE area (for instance, legal, accounting, weight loss, retail, relationship counseling, marketing, funnels, etc.).

Examples of ONE area of expertise aka niche market (NM):

For service providers/entrepreneurs:

- Business
- Financial
- Personal development
- Health industry

For professionals:

- Legal
- Accounting
- Real estate

For retail:

- Retail Store

EXPERT DECLARATION

Once you determine your area of expertise (NM), then declare your specific expert title. Put your stake in the ground in this specific area. Muhammad Ali use to rant, "I am the champ," before he ever won a fight. You may or may not "feel" like an expert, but what you believe to be true is true, so you need to start declaring it NOW.

Declare who you are as an expert; then continue to grow and develop mastery along the way. It's all about declaring who you see yourself BECOMING. You must teach people how to receive you. You may not be the heavyweight champion right now, but you can declare it and grow into your heavyweight shoes.

When I took on that homicide case, it was the first murder case I signed on, but I had confidence because of the mastery and litigation experience I had developed over the years trying other serious criminal cases.

Claiming your expert title could look like this:

Area of Expertise (NM)	Expert Title
Business	Business Coach
Business	Marketing Maven
Finance	Investment Mentor
Personal Development	Life Coach
Health & Wellness	Weight Loss Queen
Legal	Trademark Lawyer
Accounting	CFO
Real Estate	Investment Broker

If you sell products or specialty services, you will likely have an industry as your niche market (NM) and a brand title/name, instead of an expert title.

Retail (NM)	Brand Title
Retail Store	Walmart
Retail Store	Saks Fifth Avenue

So, examine your area of expertise, profession, or industry (NM) and put your expert stake in the ground. If you need more clarity around determining your ITI expert factors, scan the QR code at the end of this play to get access to a free bonus, my ITI Expert Factor Worksheet.

1. Expert declaration: I am an expert in (NM) ____________
2. Put your stake in the ground: My expert/brand title ____________

II. Perfect Dream Client

Now that you are clear on your area of expertise/industry (NM) and expert/brand title, the next question to focus on is who is the person or specific market that benefits most from your area of expertise? I want you to think of ONE person or ONE market. There is someone in the marketplace suffering from a problem you have an expert solution for, and you need to get clear on who this person/market is.

This person might have even been *you* a few years back. Think of when you had a big problem and how you solved it for yourself—for example, you may have lost weight, thrived after a divorce, or changed careers.

This person or market could also be suffering from a problem you solved in the past for someone else—maybe you helped someone else lose weight, recover after a divorce, or get a promotion. It could also be someone suffering with a problem you have skill and specialized training in (ex: tax preparation, tax planning, real estate investing, litigation). We will get into the problem next, but for now, let's focus on identifying that one person or market that you can help. This is often referred to as your "niche." I refer to this person/market segment as your "Perfect Dream Client" (PDC) or your "Perfect Dream Client Avatar."

Once again, remember the rule of ONE. You must choose ONE PDC. This will allow you to develop mastery and become the go-to expert for that specific PDC. They say there are "riches in niches."

The clearer you can get on your PDC, the richer you can be—so let's get *super* clear!

Pick a PDC

Here's what it could look like so far.

Area of Expertise (NM)	**Expert Title**	**PDC (Niche)**
Business	Business Coach	Women Entrepreneurs
Finance	Investment Mentor	High Income Earners
Personal Development	Life Coach	Careeer Women
Health & Wellness	Weight Loss Queen	Overweight Women
Profession (NM) (General Area)	**Expert Title (Your Specialty)**	**PDC (Niche) (Your Specific Client Type)**
Legal	IP Attorney	Trademark Clients

Legal	Criminal Defense Attorney	Criminal Defendants
Accounting	CPA	Tax Planning Clients
Real Estate	Investment Broker	Real Estate Investor
Retail (NM)	**Brand Title**	**PDC (Niche)**
Retail Store	Walmart	bargain shoppers
Retail Store	Neiman Marcus	Luxury Shoppers

The more you niche down, the easier it is to address your PDC when you speak and market to them.

Exception: When starting out in business as a professional, be careful of going from a niche market to a specialized niche too soon. For example, accountants can serve business owners when they start their business journey: that could be your niche market. Later you may only do accounting for a specific PDC—for instance, nonprofits or real estate investors. In the beginning of your business journey, you may have to work with enough people to stay in business and to get to know who you prefer working with in the future when you are ready to narrow your niche.

Picking one PDC will allow you to gain mastery, build a "known for" reputation, and demand premium prices. Remember, specialists tend to be more highly valued and attract more interest than generalists; that's why there are riches in niches. Having one PDC will allow you to focus all of your messaging and marketing on just one niche.

Only promote to one niche. You cannot market to everyone. When you promote and speak to "everyone" you are essentially promoting and speaking to "no one." When you speak on stage, write content, and create marketing assets, you should be speaking to ONE person, you may attract more and that's fine, but the point of having one PDC is to keep you focused on only purposely attracting that one type of person. A lux shopper can go to Walmart and if they walk out, Walmart doesn't care: they aren't Walmart's PDC/target customer anyhow. If they purchase, great! Walmart is happy to do business with them even though they don't market to them.

The key is to remember that you are in a client-centered business, which means everything you do is driven by the needs, problems, and desires of your perfect dream clients; therefore, you should only focus on attracting that one PDC. This is common in every market.

Now that you have identified the one person or market you will serve, your PDC, let's go into a deeper analysis of who this PDC really is.

PDC ARCHETYPE

It is important that you get really clear on all the attributes of your PDC. You must examine the internal, external, and geographic attributes of the PDC you plan to attract.

Creating a PDC avatar archetype is a great way to go deeper into the attributes of your PDC—here's a way to start brainstorming and understanding what they're all about.

Here are three areas to explore:

1. **Demographics (external attributes)** – What is their gender, age, education, income, employment and career?

2. **Psychographics (internal attributes)** – What are their personality, beliefs, values, likes, and dislikes? You must get

in their head to successfully market to them because, after all, people buy based on emotions. Your PDC will buy your expert solution if they like you, afterwards they will use logic to justify the purchase. People will talk themselves into working with you or out of working with you. Psychographics will help you understand this decision-making process.

3. **Geographics (location attributes)** – Where is your PDC located? You need to know where they hang out and network (for instance, which social network are they using, do they often hold events in your area, etc.). Geographics will tell you where to find them.

It may be helpful to write out a paragraph with all the attributes of your PDC. I even have my clients find a picture of their PDC and give their PDC a name to make this PDC avatar more real so you can visualize this person every time you market to them.

Now that you know your niche market, expert (or brand) title, know who you will serve (PDC) and all your PDC's attributes, it's time to uncover their problems.

III. Pressing Problem that you'll Solve - Urgency is Key

Get clear on your PDC's pressing problem, urgent problem that needs solving (UPS). Again, remember the rule of one: you want to uncover their problems so you can focus on and solve their ONE biggest and most urgent problem because this is what is giving them their biggest pain.

Your PDC will usually pay you for a solution to an urgent problem they need to solve. For example, if they are having cash flow problems, they will pay you if you can help them have consistent cashflow (their desire) and finally sleep peacefully without worrying about paying bills. Or if they are overweight and at risk of a heart attack, they have an urgent need to lose weight, and will be more likely to pay someone to help them achieve their pressing weight loss goal.

You must determine your PDC's pressing problem. When analyzing your PDC's problems, ask yourself:

- What problem is my PDC suffering with?
- Is this an urgent problem?
- Does it involve one of these three key areas?
    - **Health**: Will improve their health or prevent illness?
    - **Wealth**: Will improve their financial situation or save them money?
    - **Relationship**: Could it help to start, improve, or end a relationship?

These are three key areas where you will often find their urgent problems that need solving (UPSs). Most people will pay money to fix a big problem in one of these three areas.

It doesn't matter if you sell a service or product, you must get clear on:

1. Your Area of Expertise (Niche Market – NM) and Your Expert /Brand Title
2. The person you will serve (PDC)
3. The urgent problem you solve (UPS)
4. Your PDC's ability to pay you for your solution

If you have a PDC (niche) with an urgent problem needing solving (UPS) who has resources to pay you and is willing to pay you, you have a viable PDC and can monetize your intellect by solving their UPS in exchange for money.

Let's map out some examples:

Area of Expertise (NM)	**Expert/ Brand Title**	**PDC**	**Urgent Problem to Solve (UPS)**	**Have $**	**Willing to Pay $**
Business	Business Strategist	Women Entrepreneurs	Cash Flow	Yes	Yes
Finance	Investment Mentor	Investors	Making Wise Investments	Yes	Yes
Accounting	CPA	Corporations	Tax Savings	Yes	Yes
Personal Development	Life Coach	Career Moms	Balancing Parenting Time	Yes	Yes
Health	Weight Loss Queen	Overweight Women	Losing Weight	Yes	Yes
Relationships	Divorce Mentor	Divorced Women	Find True Soul Mate	Yes	Yes
Legal	IP Lawyer	Business Owners	Theft of Brand	Yes	Yes
Retail	Shopify Specialust	Online Store Owners	Getting Clients	Yes	Yes

Here's what mine looks like today:

Area of Expertise (NM)	**Expert/ Brand Title**	**PDC (Niche)**	**Problem (UPS)**	**Have $**	**Willing to Pay $**
Business	Business Growth Strategist	Professionals/ Entrepreneurs (YOU)	Monetizing Their Intellect	Yes	Yes

I have a viable PDC!

Map this out for yourself. Confirm YOU have a viable PDC before moving forward.

Once you have a viable PDC (your ideal customer or client), you must learn how to communicate with them in a magnetic way.

IV. Instant Attraction—Your magnetizing marketing message (MMM)

Once you determine you have a viable PDC, you must learn how to communicate with your PDC in a magnetic way.

Create a "Dog Whistle" for your PDC

Imagine it's late at night. You're driving home along a dark highway. You hear a noise, and your car starts to drive weirdly. You pull over and see that you have a flat tire. You look around, and all you see is a dark wooded area. You are alone. You check your trunk, and you locate the spare, but the jack is missing. You recall previously taking it out of the trunk to lend to a friend, but you don't recall putting it back. You must have forgotten. You frantically call for roadside assistance.

First, you call Babble Tow Company. The following conversation transpires:

Babble Tow: *"Good evening, how can we help you?"*

Scared Stranded Driver: *"I just had a tire blow out. I'm on the side of the road in what appears to be no man's land. I don't have a jack to change my tire, but I have a spare. Can you please help me ASAP?"*

Babble Tow: *"Sure, we specialize in situations like this. I will send my roadside mechanic out with our special hydro plane jack lifting machine.*

He will check the compression of your spare tire, then use our advanced jack machine to get your vehicle lifted with precise measurements. He will then assess the situation and proceed to change the blown-out tire with the spare you have. So long as he doesn't encounter any additional issues, he should be able to replace your damaged tire with your spare. Would you like me to send the roadside mechanic out?"

Now imagine this conversation:

Safe Driver Towing: *"Good evening, are you in a safe location?"*

Scared Stranded Driver: *"Yes, I just had a tire blow out. I'm on the side of the road in what appears to be no man's land. I don't have a jack to change my tire, but I have a spare. Can you please help me ASAP?"*

Safe Driver Towing: *"Sure, I've just tracked your location and can have a roadside specialist to you momentarily. He can be there in 10 minutes or less. He will have you back on the road in no time so you can get home safely, and in time to enjoy dinner with your family. Would you like me to dispatch our roadside specialist?"*

Which company are you likely to select? You probably couldn't care less about the process described by Babble Towing and feel better about the answer offered by Safe Driver Towing because their messaging was directed at your "desired result", getting home safely. Safe Driver Towing provided clearer messaging and gave you the best answer to ease your fears at that time.

Your Magnetic Marketing Message (MMM):

When speaking to your PDC, you must speak clearly in a way that resonates with their desired result. They don't care about your tools, techniques, and/or processes, like Babble Tow Company's mumbo jumbo. But they do care about you solving their problem and making them feel better, as Safe Driver Towing did.

When you initially communicate with your PDC, you only have a few minutes (possibly seconds) to grab their attention, so you must deliver magnetic marketing messaging (MMM).

Here are a few samples of MMM—choose the version that you resonate with the most:

1. I help (**Perfect Dream Client)** get/solve **(Urgent Problem needing Solving**).

   Example 1: I help disabled motorists get back on the road safely.

   Example 2: I help overweight women lose 30 pounds.

2. I help (**PDC**) get/solve **(UPS**) so they can (**Desired Outcome**).

   Example 1: I help disabled motorists get back on the road safely so they can get to their destination.

   Example 2: I help overweight women lose 30 pounds in 30 days so they can fit back into their favorite skinny jeans.

3. **(PDC)** hires me to get/solve (**UPS**).

   Example 1: Small business owners making $100,000 a year or more hire me to reduce their tax liability.

4. (**PDC**) hires me to get/solve (**UPS**) so they can (**Desired Outcome**).

   Example 1: Small business owners making $100,000 a year or more hire me to reduce their tax liability so they can have more money to put toward their retirement.

Your MMM must hit your PDC in the heart—NOT the head—so don't babble on!

V. Create a PDC Envision Board

Once you know your niche market, expert title, your PDC, their attributes and problems, and how to communicate with them in a way that brings instant attraction through your MMM, you can create a Client Envision Board. This will give you a clear picture of where your client is now, where they will be after working with you, and how you will get them from A to B.

You want to make sure your expert solution or product will be the bridge between where your PDC is now and where they will be after experiencing your expert solution. An Envision Board is meant to help you clearly envision exactly what your solution will look like.

Here is an example of a PDC Envision Board:

Life before experiencing your service or product	Life after experiencing your service or product
Pain	Gain
Feeling	Feeling
Typical Day	Typical Day
State	State

Mapping before and after scenarios out will help you get clarity on where your PDC is, how your product/service will help them, and where they will be after working with you. This also gives you more clarity when communicating with them. Moreover, it will help you build the bridge between where they are and where they will be after experiencing your product/service. We will build the bridge that will bring them their desired result in the next play.

Let's Make the Second Play

You are now ready to be the attractive EPPIC expert in your business.

Implement The Second Play, and then complete the checklist:

1. **E**xpert Declaration – Determine your niche market and expert title:
   Niche market________ and Expert Title___________

2. **P**erfect Dream Client – Identify your one PDC and his/her attributes _______
3. **P**roblem you solve – Identify your PDC's biggest urgent problem needing solving (UPS) ______ and if they are ready, willing, and able to pay for your expert solution _______
4. **I**nstant Attraction – Magnetic Marketing Messaging – Create your MMM ______
5. **C**reate Your Client Envision Board ______

If you've completed the checklist…

Congratulations!

You have established yourself as the attractive EPPIC expert in your business and **Pillar #2 - Attraction** is in place.

Listen to my personal message and download a free copy of my ITI expert factor worksheet by scanning the code with your smartphone or go to:

https://www.intellecttoincome.com/playtwoitifactor

The Third Play

"Freedom Framework"

Profit Pillar #3 –
Create a Signature Offer System

"Did I just make six figures in 60 minutes?"
... the leverage aha moment!

The Road to Leverage

I was enjoying the fruits of my labor. Being positioned as the attractive EPPIC expert in my law firm allowed me to expand my firm to three locations in the first year. I was generating multiple six figures. The transition from being a commodity in the workplace to an attractive EPPIC expert in the legal marketplace was paying off. Life was great. After several years of operating my law firm and taking on business and criminal clients, I wrote my first book, *SOAR: Beyond the Heels of Adversity*, which resulted in many speaking opportunities. Those speaking opportunities led to a side hustle coaching/consulting business for entrepreneurs.

As my speaking opportunities grew, so did my coaching/consulting business. I eventually stopped taking criminal cases. It became literally impossible to do. I could no longer run from courthouse-to-courthouse handling cases, or from jail to jail visiting incarcerated clients. I enjoyed working with entrepreneurs so much and developed a strong passion in this area. I became the attractive EPPIC expert in my coaching and consulting business.

I started magnetically attracting professionals and entrepreneurs. As a result, I shifted my focus toward only working with entrepreneurs and professionals in both my law firm and my coaching/consulting business. My law firm niched down to providing business and trademark services only. McPherson IP Law helps entrepreneurs protect their business, brand, and profit so they can make more money and keep it.

My coaching and consulting business helps entrepreneurs and professionals monetize their intellect by launching, growing, and scaling lucrative lifestyle businesses (that are legally protected) so you can have more time, location, and financial freedom. Building this business was a perfect blending of my unique expert skills: business and legal. Speaking engagements became a big part of my coaching/consulting business.

I recall the speaking opportunity that changed the entire trajectory of my business and gave me my second aha moment. As you may recall, my first aha moment was discovering how valuable my intellect was in the marketplace outside of my employee position as a prosecutor. Realizing I had a unique skillset took me from commodity to expert. Moving from commodity to an attractive EPPIC expert allowed me to generate $50,000 for one case, instead of nearly $50,000 working as a prosecutor all year. Elevating from a workplace commodity to a valuable expert in the marketplace was enlightening.

But that was just the beginning…

It was November 17, 2020. I was scheduled to speak virtually to a group of entrepreneurs. By this time I had had so many speaking engagements, nationally and internationally, I considered myself a pro, so I was not nervous about the speaking itself. But I was a bit anxious still because this talk was different: for the first time, I'd be making a paid offer at the end of the speaking session. I had a digital course that I had created while coaching my private clients and had sold a few on webinars, but today was a big opportunity. I would offer my digital product to a huge audience.

I remember logging on to my computer. I saw there were about 300 entrepreneurs logged on. The host introduced me. She read my bio, citing all my degrees, education, and experience. (I was like *wow; I really am an attractive expert character*!) She highlighted all my expertise, talked about my work, freedom, and travel lifestyle, and then mentioned her personal relationship with me. She had the audience fired up, eager to welcome me to the stage. I took the virtual stage and spoke for nearly 60 minutes. I told my hero's journey story: how I went from struggling teenage mom to accomplished attorney and successful business mentor. I then taught three of my five legal pillars for protecting your business, brand, and profit. I had a sense that I had deeply connected with the audience.

During my talk, the audience appeared to be very engaged. They laughed at my jokes, nodded when I spoke directly to them, and applauded when I finished. At the end of my talk, I made a call to action—an opportunity for the audience to learn and get more help from me. I offered my Legally Bossed Up Bootcamp, my signature digital course, for a special event price of $997. I ended my talk with this: "I could not cover all of my Legal Pillars in this short talk, but my program, *Legally Bossed Up Bootcamp: The Ultimate Legal Program for Entreprenuers*, will walk you step by step through all five of my proven Legal Pillars. So, if you are ready to get legally bossed up, click the link in the chat to get started at the special event-only price."

My team dropped the purchase link in the chat, and what happened next was amazing. Over 70 people clicked the link immediately, purchasing my product. I then invited those with questions to my virtual speaking booth where not only did more click the link, but two attendees also later joined my $7,500 group coaching program.

That 60-minute talk generated over six figures! I thought to myself, *did I just make six figures from a 60-minute talk?*

To say this was an aha moment is an understatement!

At that moment, I realized my intellect was not only valuable in the marketplace, but it was also LEVERAGEABLE! I thought back to my prosecutor days when I traded time for money and was earning $48,000 a year. I then thought back to my criminal defense days when I took my intellect directly to the marketplace and could demand $50,000 for one case. However, not every client paid me $50,000, and one case could take months or years to conclude. But the fact was, I just generated what I would in two years as a prosecutor and what I could for one case that took years to resolve from a 60-minute talk, and there was zero follow-up work to be done. WOW!

Repeat after me:

"LEVERAGE IS THE PROFIT PATHWAY TO A LUCRATIVE LIFESTYLE BUSINESS!"

I had just sat in my home office dressed up from the waist up with slippers on and ultimately generated $100,000 from a 60-minute talk. Let that resonate for a second... *that's* what is possible when you turn your intellect to income and LEVERAGE it. At that moment, I realized I needed to monetize more of THAT and less of the other stuff I was slaving over. If I did those talks ten times a year, that's a million-dollar business. So, I began doing just that: traveling the world and speaking to entrepreneurs on how to get Legally Bossed Up.

Everything about this was a win-win experience. I got to enjoy beautiful destinations, meet awesome business owners, and live life on my terms. And my audience got their legal foundation in place so they could go on to make more money and protect their businesses. Many entrepreneurs saw what I was doing—traveling to beautiful locations and speaking to large audiences—and they started asking me to help them do the same. So, I decided to leverage my intellect on another platform, a group program.

Soon after, I launched my Intellect to Income Group Coaching Program where I take my clients through my **LACED**™ method, showing them the exact roadmap I use to leverage my expertise so they can have a lucrative lifestyle business doing what they love. I teach my clients how this is possible and the secret sauce behind leverage, a Signature Offer System.

Signature Offer System

A Signature Offer System (SOS) is your freedom framework. It is the key to a successful lifestyle business. I was able to generate six figures from a 60-minute talk because of my SOS. Every entrepreneur should have an SOS. You are not a "wingman," so you should not be "winging it" with your clients! A proven, unique framework is the foundation to getting your clients results.

My SOS framework is the LACED Method™. I do not offer ANYTHING outside of this framework. When you have a framework in place, you can create an offer suite of your products and services. Your product offer suite is the bread and butter of your business. Your lead magnets (free introductory offers), signature talks, products, and services will all stem from your SOS framework, the foundation of your product offer suite. Having an SOS makes creating offers easy-breezy. This process is a game changer.

The PDC Envision Board you created in The Second Play can help you map this out. When you know what your PDC's problems and desires are, and you have the expertise to take your PDC from where they are to where they want to be, you can build a very successful lifestyle business around this intellect. Your SOS framework is the bridge your PDC will travel to get to their desired result.

A Signature Offer System (SOS) "WINS"™ every time!

Your SOS is the bridge for taking your PDC from pain island to pleasure island.

It is your process, your proprietary method. You must have a proven system to get your PDC results.

Benefits of an SOS:

- Allows you to become organized, confident, and prepared (versus winging it).

- Helps you create offers with ease and helps your PDC ascend your Offer Value Ladder (OVL)—the OVL staircase is your product suite.

- Allows you to create various delivery formats from your mapped-out method, making it easier for you to meet your PDC where they are and serve them from that place. (Examples: lead magnets for initial awareness, books for low-level entry, courses as mid-ticket offerings, high-ticket offers like 1:1 sessions, group programs, and masterminds for those higher up on the OVL staircase.)

- Allows you to build a sustainable business–An SOS system allows you to not only serve your PDC at every level but nurture them to get to your higher ticket offers. This leads to business sustainability.

- Helps mastery set in so you can become an expert in your niche–Specialized knowledge leads to premium pricing (remember, mastery = money… *cha-ching*!)

- Allows you to price for value, not time–You have a predictable system proven to get results, so you no longer question the value and get stuck with pricing.

- Allows you to make money when needed by quickly creating an offer. For instance, you can pull from your signature offer system and do a challenge, a webinar, a podcast, a speaking gig, an online program, and/or create a packaged product.

- It becomes your proven process and ultimate freedom framework!

An SOS is the Proven Path to Profit

A proven SOS is the path I use and teach my clients to use to create consistent cash flow. Having an SOS allowed me to package my

LACED Method™ into a digital product and generate six figures from a 60-minute talk. That is the power of a solid SOS. Creating YOUR signature system based off of your intellect can position you to do the same thing.

My proprietary SOS, the LACED Method™, is premised upon my intellect: my degrees, education, experience, and training in legal and business. I also interviewed and worked with clients and learned about their struggles. After declaring my area of expertise in legal and business, I identified professional service providers/entrepreneurs as my PDCs. I identified their biggest problem: making money and keeping it. I then created an Envision Board and mapped out my SOS to address this UPS, hence the LACED Method™ was born.

LACED METHOD™ (based on my client's UPS)

- L- **Legalize** – My PDC had no idea how to protect their business, brand, and profits.
- A- **Attraction** – My PDC did not know how to consistently attract clients.
- C- **Creation of an SOS** – My PDC did not have a signature framework for offer creation and leverage.
- E- **Enrollment** – My PDC was struggling to close sales and handle objections.
- D- **Design a scale system** – My PDC was stuck growing and scaling.

I combined my legal and business education, background, and experience to create my unique framework, and I do not offer any services outside of my expert framework.

Creating Your SOS

Your unique combination of degree(s), education, experiences, training, and/or intellect can be used to create an SOS to deliver your expert solution to your PDC. Your unique methodology will further position you as an expert and differentiate you from other experts. It is therefore imperative that you have an SOS.

Once you identify your PDC and their UPS, you can create a framework—a solution "bridge"—to bring them from pain island (where they are when you meet them) to pleasure island (where they will be after experiencing your expert solution). When you have a unique proven framework, it creates WINS for you and your PDC because there is certainty; it becomes your proven path to get results for your clients. Here's how to create your unique SOS framework using my WINS formula:

1. **W**rite: Write out your step-by-step process, in the exact order your client must go through to achieve their desired result. This step-by-step process can be 3, 5, 7, or 10 steps; the sweet spot is 3 to 5 steps. I recommend 5 or 6 as ideal. Three may not be enough, and 10 may be overload.

   For example, my LACED Method™, my Signature Framework, is the exact process I take my clients through. It has 5 steps and I often teach 3 of my 5 steps (pillars) on webinars and talks leaving more to be desired by my PDC and a reason to invest in my call to action.

   Brainstorm your step-by-step process, your signature framework, as you move on to the next step.

2. **I**dentify and bridge the gap: Identify the pain and desired outcomes. Then create the content you will teach to bridge the gap under each step in your framework.

   Example: This is how my framework addresses my PDC's pain and desired outcome.

   i. Pain – The pain/problem they have before investing in my solution.

      - **L** – Fear of the unknown—Business, brand, and profit at risk and no idea what's needed on the legal side of the business
      - **A** – Worrying about how to get more clients, struggling to attract PDCs
      - **C** – Cash flow crisis—not making consistent offers or generating consistent income
      - **E** – Not closing enough sales, struggling to convert prospects into clients
      - **D** – Not growing and scaling, stuck trying to take the business to the next level

   ii. The solution/desired outcome

      - **L** – Legalize—legal protection
      - **A** – Attracting lots of viable PDCs
      - **C** – Consistent cash flow
      - **E** – Enrolling more prospects into clients
      - **D** – A designed system for growing and scaling with ease

   iii. Bridge the gap: The content to teach so your PDC reaches the desired outcome.

Example of my LACED Method™ content/sub-frameworks

a. **L** – My five foundational Legal Pillars (SCIIP)
b. **A** – Attraction–Expert positioning for magnetic client attraction (EPPIC)
c. **C** – Creation of a Signature Offer System (WINS)
d. **E** – Enrollment conversations and objection handling (MOST)
e. **D** – Design a scale system (SCALE)

Brainstorm your PDCs pains, desired outcomes, and the content (sub-frameworks) you will teach to bring them from their pain island to gain island.

3. **N**ame your signature offer system – If you can come up with an acronym/hook after reviewing your process, great. If not, just pick a name that relates to the promised outcome. Always choose clear over clever. Example of my name: The LACED Method™–Every business needs to be LACED up.

   Brainstorm what you will name your SOS and

   Brainstorm what you will name your SOS sub-frameworks

4. **S**ervice Delivery–Choose the best service delivery format: 1:1, group, online program, VIP Day, retreat—as you grow and scale you will add other service delivery options, but always start with ONE.

Once you create your SOS, you can choose various service delivery formats.

I created an SOS framework, the LACED Method™, from my intellect. My LACED Method™ framework allows me to create various offer formats. I was able to put my framework content in the format of a book that I sell to the masses, digital courses that I sell to the masses, a group coaching program that allows me to enroll and serve many, and live events that allow me to enroll many into my group program, mastermind, or retreat.

Example of my various SOS formats:

Legally Bossed UP

Book: *Legally Bossed Up: The Ultimate Legal Playbook*
Workbook: *Legally Bossed Up: The Ultimate Legal Play Workbook*
Digital Course: Legally Bossed Up Bootcamp: The Premier Legal Training for Entrepreneurs

Intellect to Income

Book: *Intellect to Income: The Ultimate Profit Playbook*
Workbook: *Intellect to Income: The Ultimate Profit Play Workbook*
Digital Course: Intellect to Income: Digital Course Made Simple
VIP Annual Membership Program: Legally Bossed Up VIP Membership Group
Group Coaching Program: Intellect to Income: Signature Group Program
Live Event: Intellect to Income Live*:* Virtual and In-Person Events

Once you have a signature offer system, you can present the same framework, in different formats — no more creating new content topics or winging it.

If you need help brainstorming your SOS, scan the QR code at the end of this play to access a free bonus, my SOS Brainstorming Worksheet.

Delivering Your SOS

As you can see, once you create a signature offer system, the only decision left is to pick a format for your offer. The platform can be a book, signature talk, digital program, group program, mastermind, retreat, or live event. If you are looking to leverage your income, select a leveraged format: book, digital course, group program, or mastermind. When you first start out, you should start with a non-leveraged platform to get proof of concept before leveraging. If you are confident in your EPPIC expertise and decide to go straight to a launch format offer, I highly recommend starting with a small beta group.

Remember the rule of one — pick one initial delivery method or offer format in the beginning. When you are ready you can teach your SOS from other formats (various offers), which is the beauty of having a signature offer system.

Once you have created an SOS, you never struggle to teach new content. Teach the content from various parts of your SOS. Teach the same content topics in different formats, with different access levels. The more direct access to you, the greater the investment.

SOS in the form of packages, memberships, and subscriptions.

Packages, memberships, and subscriptions will ALWAYS produce more profit than one-off sells. It doesn't matter if you are offering coaching, consulting or professional services such as legal, dental, fitness, lash, makeup, massage, chiropractic or more, your SOS may be packaged into a bundle. You should offer packages or subscriptions rather than one-off services for greater leveraged income.

You can use the WINS method to create packages:

1. Write out the number of packages you will have – ex. 3
2. Identify the services that will be in the packages
3. Name your packages - ex. Bronze, Gold, and Platinum
4. Select your Service delivery format – ex. In store or online

Packages Example:

Dentist Packages
Bronze – X-ray and cleaning
Gold – X-ray–cleaning–whitening
Platinum – X-ray, cleaning, whitening, veneers
Service Delivery Format: In Office

Fitness Center Packages
Bronze – Weekday gym access
Gold – Unlimited gym access and basic nutrition plan
Platinum – Unlimited gym access, customized nutrition plan, personal trainer access, 1 free guest pass
Service Delivery Format: In Gym

Wax, Nail, Massage, or Lash Center Packages
Bronze – Monthly service, one free service after every 10 services
Gold – Monthly service, two free services after every 10 services and 1 free product per month
Platinum – Monthly service, two free services after every 10 services, access to wine and juice bar during services, 1 free guest pass every 60 days
Service Delivery Format: In Salon/Studio

Here's what an SOS can look like:

An SOS is the foundation of a profitable offer system that will allow you to create a product suite—it's the gift that keeps on giving!

So let's create your SOS framework.

Let's Make the Third Play

You are now ready to create your proprietary SOS using my WINS method.

Implement The Third Play, and then complete the checklist.

Step 1: **W** – Write out the step-by-step process, in the exact order, you will take your PDC to go from pain to gain so they achieve their desired result _____

Step 2: **I** – Identify the pains (UPS) and gains (desired outcomes) under each step and then create content to bridge the gap between identified pains and gains. _____

Step 3: **N** – Name your SOS—remember, clear over clever _____

Step 4: **S** – Select the offer format you plan to deliver the solution in (a book, product, coaching program, package, talk, etc.) Remember, start with ONE offer format and as you grow you can add more offers to your product suite. _____

If more appropriate for your business, create an SOS bundle of your product or services:

Bronze _______
Silver _______
Platinum _______
Service Delivery Format _______

If you've completed the checklist...

Congratulations!

You have created your Freedom Framework
and Profit Pillar #3
Your Signature Offer System is in place.

Listen to my personal message and download a free copy of my SOS brainstorming worksheet by scanning the code above with your smartphone or go to:

https://www.intellecttoincome.com/playthreesos

The Fourth Play

"Prospects to Client"

Profit Pillar #4 – Enrollment

"Buy my Shi!"*
...the awkward sales call...YIKES!

The Power of Serving Over Selling

My SOS has allowed me to consistently enroll clients into my business. Converting prospects into clients is an artform that I've learned to master. I've been selling my services seamlessly since my litigation attorney days, so selling comes naturally to me, but I've learned that it doesn't come so naturally for everyone.

Shortly after speaking at the event where I sold my Legally Bossed Up Bootcamp, I attended a live event and went to a breakout session on hosting events; the speaker (we'll call her Nancy), was awesome. At the end of the event, Nancy offered complimentary calls to the attendees. I accepted and booked. I was looking forward to speaking to her. She offers event hosting services, and I was interested in hosting my next event so I thought it would be great to hear a different perspective.

On the day of the scheduled call, Nancy called me, and the conversation went sort of like this:

"Hi Shevelle, it was great connecting with you at the event. I am glad you booked a call to chat further. Are you thinking of hosting an event any time soon?"

I replied, "Yes, I am."

She said, "Great." She went on to explain the features of her event program and how she helps entrepreneurs launch successful events. She talked about the particulars and duration of her event program. She then went into further detail about the action I needed to take in the program. She explained that I would begin by flying to Miami to meet with her for a daylong, in-person planning session. She then described the curriculum of the planning session and all that I would be required to do.

The more she talked about "all I had to do," I just cringed. I was ready to end the call soon after it began but I let her do her spiel. I was not receiving any value; I was not interested in doing "all the work" she described at length, and I did not feel an emotional desire to buy anything from her. She then went into her pricing and payment plans and concluded by asking me if I would like to join her program. I politely declined.

She asked if there was something she missed or if I had any questions. I said: "Nope, you covered it all," and I hung up. The fact was she did cover it all, all of the details and features of her program, but she did not cover anything I needed to hear to get me inspired or even interested in enrolling in her program.

Don't be like Nancy!

No one wants to be sold to, but everyone wants to be served.

All Nancy did was try to sell me a program without serving me. She didn't inquire about what *"I"* wanted. People tend to listen to one "radio station," which I call WIIFM (what's in it for me). They don't care about you or your program. Most of the time they don't even care about what they need… they only care about what they WANT.

I tell my clients all the time: "Sell them what they *want*; then give them what they *need* in your service or product." If Nancy had inquired about what "*I*" wanted, she would have learned that I wanted to host a profitable event at a beautiful location, preferably by a beach. Upon hearing this, she could have solely focused on that alone. If she had opened up the floor for me to do the talking and for her to do the listening, she would have learned what my desires were and honed in on that. She missed out on hearing what she needed to center the call around: my desires. Had she not missed out on this, she could have talked about how her program could 10x my event profit and be held at a beautiful beach resort.

Just letting me know that she could get me that result would have been music to my ears, and I would have likely enrolled in her program. Once enrolled, she could have then provided me with all the details of how the program works and what I needed to do next, either after the call or in the onboarding process. I wouldn't have cared about doing the work at that point because I would have already been sold on getting what I *want* as a result of doing that work.

So, when enrolling your PDC, you must be a private investigator and find out what they want. Listen, listen, listen, and then show them how your product or service will get them the exact result they want.

Here's another example:

The Cell Phone Upgrade Sales Call:

I received a telephone call from a cell phone company representative named Blunt. It went like this:

Blunt: *"Hello Shevelle, I'm reaching out to you because we just launched the latest iPhone. You are due for an upgrade. Would you be interested in upgrading?"*

My immediate response was *"No."* and I hung up.

I am not the person who runs out and buys a new gadget because the latest version is coming out. In fact, I will use my phone until the numbers fall off. My motto is: *"If it ain't broke, I ain't fixing it!"*

But then I get this call about the same upgrade from a representative named Smooth:

Smooth: *"Hello Shevelle, how are you?"*

Me: *"I am great."*

Smooth: *"That is great. So, I'm just calling to check in with you to see how you are doing and how business is going?"*

Me: *"Business is great. I've been busy traveling a lot lately."*

Smooth: *"That sounds amazing, what's been your favorite place visited so far?"*

Me: *"Bali, hands down."*

Smooth: *"Yes, I heard Bali is beautiful. I bet you took some awesome photos."*

Me: *"A few. I wish I had hired a professional photographer looking back. I could have gotten some great lifestyle photos for my business."*

Smooth: *"What type of business do you have?"*

Me: *"A coaching/consulting business, and more lifestyle photos would have been great."*

Smooth: *"Oh, yes, I can see how lifestyle photos would be perfect for your business. Do you have an iPhone?"*

Me: *"Yes."*

Smooth: *"What version do you have?"*

Me: *"I don't even know… I don't keep up. As long as it works, I'm good!"*

Smooth: *"Oh, I understand, I was just asking because the latest version takes the most AMAZING pictures. It was just released, and the quality is equivalent to that of a professional camera. The camera has improved 10x since the last version. I had the old model and I swear I had to take at least 10 selfies, just to get one good one. I am so psyched that I don't have to do that anymore. It's one and done with this iPhone camera. It is so sharp and precise. My friend Sasha just came back from Aruba, and her pictures are 10 times better than the photos from her last trip. The camera's improvement is MIND BLOWING. The photos look like they were taken by a professional."*

Me: *"Oh really?"* (The salesperson now has my attention because she's talking about WIIFM.)

Yes: *"Are you doing a lot more traveling anytime soon?"*

Me: *"Yes, I'm going to Paris and Dubai next month."*

Smooth: *"Oh, more beautiful places. I bet you want to capture those moments and create not only great memories but get great pictures for your social media, webinars, and events. That would be great for your type of business. With a great iPhone camera that has great precision, a sharp lens, and a countdown timer coupled with a tripod, you can take AMAZING lifestyle pictures yourself."*

Me: *"That sounds awesome!"*

Smooth: *"The next generation iPhone sounds perfect for you. You can capture those lifestyle photos with professional photography quality without having to hire a photographer everywhere you travel. What more can you ask for? You'll have professional lifestyle photos without the cost and hassle of finding a photographer. Plus, there's a special promo for those who upgrade on the call, you get a FREE travel tripod—the same one my friend Sasha bought for $75 and used to take those beautiful pictures in Aruba."*

Me: *"I would love to be able to capture those beautiful moments on the fly. Can you tell me more about this iPhone and how I can get one?"*

Boom–Smooth is smooth! She has my full attention, and now I'm asking for more…

Do you see the difference? I didn't want to be *sold* an iPhone, but Smooth was serving me up all the reasons why I should have one. She learned of ONE pain point I had, not getting professional photos, she focused on that pain and talked about how her product could solve my problem—she focused on what I WANTED. This is how you sell to your PDC without selling.

Conversations that Convert

Now that you have an SOS and can create and sell a product or service, you need to know how to convert your PDC into an actual client without being "salesy" like Nancy or Blunt. You want to be a *smooth* enroller, like Smooth!

Enrollment is simply a smooth conversation that leads to an exchange of your solution for money with someone (PDC) who needs your solution to solve the urgent problem they need solved (UPS). They must be ready, willing, and able to pay for the exchange.

The main reason people say "no" is because you are trying to convince them to buy based on your reasons (those features you love to talk about) and not your PDC's reasons (the results they would love to get). That is why I said "no" to Nancy and Blunt: they kept talking about what was important to them, not me. Smooth, on the other hand, leaned into the conversation and listened to what was important to me. She then focused solely on that: my desire to have beautiful photos when I travel.

You Have a Moral Obligation to Make Offers

When you learn what your PDC is suffering with or desiring to have, and you know you have a proven solution, it would be selfish of you to not make an offer to your PDC. You are an expert and can bring transformation into your PDC's life. Whether they will buy is none of your business. Selling doesn't mean "everyone" is going to buy—sometimes people will say "no." Selling is about making offers, so they are aware of the possibility of getting your solution to solve their problem or achieve their goal. You are not in the business of "convincing" people to have something they don't want; you are in the business of identifying what they *do* want, then offering them your product or service that will give them that desired result.

Smooth made me aware of the possibility of taking great photos for my lifestyle business without the hassle and expense of hiring a professional photographer. That is all selling is, offering the possibility of something better.

What if Pfizer or Moderna didn't offer the vaccination during the Covid pandemic? That would have been devastating. Everyone did not opt to take the vaccine, and that is their choice, but Pfizer and Moderna had a moral obligation to offer it. You have a moral obligation to make offers. Be committed to making the offer, but not committed to the decision you receive.

And remember, it takes just as much energy and time to make a low-ticket offer as a high-ticket offer, so always be open to making high-ticket offers. Also remember the rule of one, you only need one thing to sell. The beauty of your SOS is that you can easily create other offers as you grow and scale. You don't have to have all your products in your offer suite ready, you just need to have ONE offer to get started.

Making sales is about mastering communication. When presenting your offer, remember to speak from the heart, not the head. You want to sell the destination, not the plane. The sales call I described with Nancy did not end with my enrollment because she NEVER sold me the destination. She kept trying to sell me the plane. People want results (more time, more money, better health, beautiful pictures), not more work (funnels, tech, systems, flying to do work, processes, and techniques).

If you want to find success turning your intellect into income, you must master the art of sales.

Mastering the Art of Sales

Your system is about taking your PDC through a process to get them a result. When selling, steer away from discussing your process, your modalities, and your systems (Babble Tow and Nancy failed because they discussed processes and systems).

Focus on the promise (the WANT), their desired destination. I consider this taking them to the Promised Land (Safe Driver Tow and Smooth did this well).

Start thinking: "I am simply offering to serve my transformation and must focus on the transformation (want/result)". I call this *enrollment.*

When you master the art of sales, it is a win-win. Your PDC needs your offer (win for them), and you need to get paid (win for you).

Listen, listen, listen...

When having enrollment conversions, the key is to listen to what your prospect WANTS. Then you can offer your solution around what they WANT (ex, Fit into skinny jeans, healthy marriage, great photographs). Once they purchase your service or product, they will get what they NEED (the modalities/your system to get the results).

Mastering communication is important because you must package your intellect into a product or service and communicate to your PDC the value it will bring. Once you package your intellect into a product or service, you can sell it on various platforms:

Virtual and live stages
Live events
Podcast
Webinars
Business expos
Your events
Sales calls
Online store

I have a simple Enrollment Method that will help you get the MOST success out of your sales conversations:

The MOST Enrollment Method

1. **M**indset: You have to shift into a service mindset. Sales is simply offering to serve your transformation. It doesn't mean your PDC will want it or will buy it. Just put yourself in a service mindset. You are simply on the call to offer your transformation (the actual results they WANT), not your *process* of getting the transformation.
   Start by meditating and clearing the pressure of selling from your mind so you can prepare to focus instead on delivering *value*. This way, the enrollment will usually follow, just like you saw in the example with Smooth.

2. **O**bjections: You must be prepared to deal with objections. Objections are excuses your PDC may have for why they can't buy your product or service.

You must learn how to overcome objections.

Here are the top 5 objections and relevant responses:

i. **Money**: "I don't have the money" is usually an excuse. You can respond by pointing out the pain they expressed and say: "It seems more like you can't afford *not* to". Discuss the opportunity cost: what is it costing your PDC to keep suffering in the pain and not experiencing the gain your product/service will bring.

   A money objection may mean you haven't tapped into enough pain. So, you can also address the pain level. *On a scale of 1–10, how important is it to you to fix the problem?* Help them see they can't afford NOT to get your transformation (for instance, they are facing a health risk your product or service can help them avoid or it can save them money such as preventing a costly divorce). You must show them that investing in your program or product will help them avoid spending more money and enduring more suffering down the road. This may cause them to become resourceful. In the previous example, Smooth addressed this by telling me how getting her product would actually SAVE me money by not needing to hire expensive photographers. She dealt with the "money" objection in her enrollment conversation. That's why knowing these objections up front can help you address them before they arise.

ii. **Permission**: "I need permission" may be something your PDC says, for instance if they feel the need to consult with a spouse or business partner. When this happens, first, make sure your PDC is sure they *want* your offer. They should be "telling" the other person why the investment needs to be made. They should be seeking the support or opinion from the other person, not asking them to make the actual decision for them. Make sure your PDC sees the value and is committed to taking action for themselves *before* consulting others. Address any questions they may have or believe the other person may want to know right away.

iii. **Time**: "I don't have time" usually points to a time management issue. Show your PDC how your product or service will save them time. Your service or product is the shortcut, the blueprint. Smooth addressed this one in her enrollment call by discussing how the new iPhone would save me the hassle (time) of searching for professional photographers every time I traveled to a different location.

iv. **No trust**: Trust can fall into three areas: They may not trust your program, themselves, or you. Here's how you deal with each area.

   a. Don't trust the program: If they say, "I don't know if this will work," you'll need to show them that this is an investment. This is the perfect opportunity to provide case studies that detail how your program works. Testimonials also provide social proof. For example, when Smooth shared the testimony of Sasha who loves her iPhone pictures from Aruba, this gave the product more credibility.

   b. Don't trust themselves: Your PDC may not trust themselves to succeed. This is where you can emphasize the support—for instance through a Facebook community, calls, accountability, etc. Smooth addressed how getting a tripod and putting on the iPhone timer would support me in taking great photos.

c. They don't trust/know/like you (yet): Show them your success, what you've done to build this successful program, and how you discovered your SOS. Smooth told me how she had to take a bunch of photos and now she doesn't with this new iPhone that takes "one and done" selfies. She shared her personal story to build trust.

iv. **No urgency**: You must point out or create urgency. Smooth created a sense of urgency by informing me there was a special promotion. This encouraged me to act fast while I was on the call to get that free tripod bonus.

Remember, your job is to deal with and overcome objections, not convince them they want something they actually don't want at all. You want to help your PDC decide yes or no. Be committed to getting them to the decision point, but not committed to the type of decision they make or the outcome of their decision. In dealing with objections, you are essentially exposing their false beliefs and unwarranted excuses. You are offering them the possibility of a better situation.

3. **S**cript: You can have a script to keep you on point but don't "be scripted." A script is for guidance, not for reading verbatim. Always be prepared to have natural conversations. Look at how natural the enrollment conversation was with

Smooth. She simply responded to my responses in a natural, relevant way.

Example – Create a simple "flow script" that will RAIISE your client up during the call (remember, it's about them NOT you):

a. **R**apport. Start by building rapport. Notice how Smooth began by saying she was just checking in and then asked how business was going. She was building rapport.

b. **A**genda. Have an agenda or goal. Smooth's agenda was to get me talking about my problem with my iPhone so she could identify one big problem (she did–camera quality) and she could serve me best on the call and then offer me a valuable solution.

c. **I**nquire. Ask, and then Listen, Listen, Listen so you can respond accordingly. After actively listening, you can then ask questions that will cause your PDC to go deeper, so you can uncover their UPS. Listen until you are clear on their UPS. Smooth did this well by listening and asking relevant follow-up questions when appropriate.

d. **I**magine. After listening until you uncover your PDC's UPS, you can then have them imagine what their future would look like once they experience the transformation of your service/product. Smooth did this well by describing how beautiful the pictures are with the new iPhone and how beautiful my pictures will be in Paris and Dubai. I started to envision my lifestyle photos taken with the new iPhone.

e. **S**hare the possibility of getting your transformation. Smooth told me about the iPhone and the bonus tripod if I act quickly.

f. **E**nroll (or **E**nd). Your PDC will usually ask how to enroll (get your product or service) if not, you can now invite them because you've done the proper serving. If for some reason, you determine during the call or at the end, they are not your PDC, simply end the conversation.

Remember to have an enrollment script, but to not be scripted. Scan the QR code at the end of this play to get access to a free bonus, my RAIISE™ Enrollment Script.

4. **T**rack Target Numbers: What isn't measured doesn't get achieved. So, it is imperative that you track your target enrollment numbers. Begin to track how many conversations you have and how many enrollments you get so you can learn and monitor your close rate to ensure consistent cash flow. How many clients you need will determine how many sales conversations you need to have.

   Example – Start by determining your income goal (e.g., $10,000 per month). If your goal is to make $10,000 this month, you have a group coaching program where you charge $2,000, and you also sell a digital course for $2,000, you need to add five clients to your group program or your digital course to hit your target income goal. If making sales calls, you may need to have 15 sales conversations if your closing rate is 30%. So, knowing your numbers is important. Your close rate will determine how many sales calls you need to regularly make (or how many live events you must participate in or host)

The Purpose of the Enrollment Conversation

The goal of the enrollment conversation is to discover your PDC's WANT so you can communicate how your service or product will give them that. This requires listening. Nancy was so busy selling, she never listened, and therefore didn't even get to hear what I wanted (to host a profitable event at a beautiful beachside location), and what was stopping me (she could have uncovered my goal and then discussed how her solution would be the bridge to get me that result). The ultimate goal is to get the person to *make a buying decision*, not to actually buy. Yes, we need to close sales but if we have smooth enrollment conversations, we don't have to focus on "selling" because the client will enroll themselves. Your role is to have a smooth enrollment conversation and be ready to receive a "Yes, I want the transformation," "No, I don't want the transformation, or "I'm not sure" (in which case you must follow up until you get a clear "no" or clear "yes").

Let's Make the Fourth Play

You are now ready to have smooth enrollment conversations.

Implement The Fourth Play, and then complete the checklist:

1. **M**indset: Determine how you will get into a "service" mindset – relax, do a breathing exercise, then choose an affirmation ___________

2. **O**bjections: Prepare and plan for how you will deal with objections _____

3. **S**cript: Have a script prepared so you can RAIISE your PDC during the call, (but make sure you don't sound like you are scripted) ____

4. **T**arget numbers: Know your target numbers so you know how many sales calls to make to hit your profit goals ____

If you completed the checklist...

Congratulations!

You are ready to have conversations that convert.

Your Profit Pillar #4 - Enrollment - is in place.

Listen to my personal message and download a free copy of my RAIISE enrollment script by scanning the code on the next page with your smartphone or go to:

https://www.intellecttoincome.com/playfourscript

The Fifth Play

"Grow and Scale"

Profit Pillar #5 – Design a SCALE System

Scaling Naturally

"Thank you for having me..."
The One-Night Stand Effect

Shortly after returning home from the event where I met Nancy, I received an invitation to speak at a women's empowerment event in New York. I read the invitation and then hopped on my computer to check out the event agenda and speaker line up, as I normally due when offered a speaker opportunity. I want to ensure the speaking opportunity is in alignment with my business scale goals.

The agenda listed some great topics of interest and some powerhouse speakers. It looked like an all-star roster. I was super excited to not only get invited to speak, but to have the opportunity to listen to the talks of so many other accomplished women. I accepted the invitation and soon after headed to New York.

I was scheduled to speak on day two, so I was thrilled to have the opportunity to go hear all of the day one speakers first. I arrived in New York the day before the event to get settled in my hotel room. The next morning I woke up bright and early. I sat on my bed reading over the itinerary marking off all of the day one speakers I wanted to hear. After I was done, I got myself ready for the day and headed down to the conference hall.

I spent the day listening to several speakers. They were all inspirational, empowering, and ended on a strong note. The really good speakers always concluded their talk with some form of invitation to get a free gift. But I specifically recall a few talks where the speakers gave great talks that ended a little differently. Those speakers ended with the same phrase: "Thank you for having me." I wanted to jump on stage and say "NOOOOOOOOO! Don't end your talk like this!"

It was like going on a hot date and not getting asked out again. No one wants to be treated like a one-night stand. It was so disappointing. What these speakers didn't realize is they were dropping the ball on scaling their business.

Scaling is not something you think about later when you decide you are ready to scale. Scaling is something you must think about at the onset. There are systems you should put in place once you start your business, so you are set up to naturally scale. Your business must have a scale method.

The S.C.A.L.E Method

The following SCALE pillars should be implemented sooner rather than later:

1. **Standard Operating Procedures** – When you are ready to build a team, you don't want to start creating your processes from scratch. I discussed this in The First Play. You should create a standard operating procedure for every task in your business so when you are at the scale level of hiring a team, you will not have to spend time training new hires, replacement hires, and virtual assistants.

2. **Calendar** – An automated calendar will allow you to pre-select your availability and provide you with a link you can give to your prospective PDCs, when you are on a podcast, at speaking events, webinars, text messages, etc. You don't want to go back and forth with others trying to find the best time to connect. Your calendar is critical to converting prospects to clients.

3. **Automation** – Automation is critical today.

   You should have the following four tasks automated:

   a. **Lead Capture** –
   You should have an automated way to collect leads in your business. Every potential PDC should be added to your email list so you can begin to nurture the relationship. You have to have a way to capture your prospects' emails so you can continue to communicate with them. This is what I wanted to jump on stage and tell those speakers that ended their talk with "Thank

you for having me." Whenever you get an opportunity to speak on stage, on a podcast, or anywhere in front of an audience, you should have a link to a free gift (a PDF checklist, guide, book—something of value to help your PDC with a UPS to get a quick win in exchange for your PDC's email). When I discuss email, you will see why this is an important part of scaling. In a nutshell, you need to collect lead information from your PDC every chance you get so you can nurture them and ultimately enroll/sell to them when they are ready to become clients/customers.

b. **Lead Conversion**

You should have automation in place to convert your prospects into clients. You should be consistently sending them automated information about business and how you are uniquely equipped to help them solve their UPS. You also want to have an automated process in place for them to easily buy your products and services. (ex: automated sales pages, video sales letters, up-sale campaigns, purchase links and a check out processes)

c. **Client Onboarding**

You should have an automated way of onboarding new clients, so they feel well taken care of. Your current clients will become the raving fans that send you referrals, so you want to start serving them with excellence from the onset. When I was in Bali, I had the opportunity to speak to a group of entrepreneurs, and I enrolled 50 clients. I generated $50,000 in 50 minutes (I love the power of leveraging my expertise!).

Here's a picture of me the next day onboarding all 50 clients:

Automation rocks!

d. **Client Service Delivery & Updates**

If any aspect of your service delivery can be automated, it should be. You should also consider automation to communicate with your clients during the client relationship. For example, in my law firm, we have automation in place to send out monthly client case status updates. The trademark process takes a year or more, and keeping clients notified consistently throughout the process creates a smooth client journey. Think of aspects of your service delivery that can and should be automated.

4. **Lifetime Learning**
   Join a community, coaching program, or mastermind. It is imperative that you keep elevating your knowledge. Experts not only master their craft, but they continue to learn and stay updated with the latest in their field.

5. **Email List Building**
   You must make growing your email list a priority. They say the money is in the list. You do not own any social media site you may advertise or post on. If that is your way of attracting and converting clients and those sites go down or disappear, so will your business if you don't build your own platform for storing your client and prospective client email addresses.

When I decided to go to Bali, I wanted to create a "Bali Fund." Because I had an email list of raving fans, I was able to invite my raven fans from my email list and host a webinar the following week that generated $10,000. This is the power of owning an email list. This is something ALL business owners need to do sooner, rather than later. It applies to plumbers, retail stores, restaurants, professional services, and entertainment. Do you know how many times I had to look up a plumber online because the last plumber was a "one and done"? He provided his service and then vanished into no man's land, never to be heard from again. That is not how you grow and scale. You need to stay in touch with past clients because they are the best source of repeat business and referrals. If you needed to raise money for a trip or an emergency, can you send out an email to your client/customer list and invite them to a webinar or a masterclass or offer them access to a sale of your merchandise or services, knowing that you will have the money you need in a few days?

If not, it's time to start building your email list. Here's how:

a. **Lead magnet delivery campaign** – Once someone gives you their email in exchange for your lead magnet, a quick solution to your PDC's problem, you need to have a campaign set up to deliver the lead magnet. For instance, if you are a health coach, you can offer your prospects a downloadable PDF on "10 Fatty Foods to Avoid" in exchange for their email. Once you deliver the free pdf, you can move them into your short-term nurture campaign.

b. **Short-term nurture campaign** – After someone new downloads your free gift, you should treat them as a hot lead by adding them to a short-term nurture campaign where you follow up with them for at least 7 days. This is typically a hot lead sequence where you are sending them emails with valuable content around their problem, attempting to convert them to a client while you are the top-of-mind expert. You want to communicate with them daily or every other day for at least 7-9 days after receiving your gift. If they don't convert into a client after these 7-9 days, you should move them into a long-term nurture campaign.

c. **Long-term nurture campaign** – Set up an email sequence to follow up periodically with those who didn't convert from your short-term email nurture campaign. This will become your general email list of non-converting PDCs; email them regularly so you remain top of mind for when they need your services. Some people on my list converted to clients years later, so nurture them and stay top of mind. This will allow you to start building an email list of potential clients that you can nurture into becoming clients/customers and ultimately raving fans and a strong referral base. Don't just email them asking them to buy your stuff—email them valuable content addressing their pain points a few times a week. Some people send daily emails, others send weekly emails—you decide, but pick a frequency and stick with it, consistency is key.

Here's what this looks like:

Again, scaling doesn't happen "suddenly." This SCALE system needs to be put in place as soon as possible so scaling will be a natural process for your business. When it's time to hire a team, run ads and take your business to the next level, you will have the foundation you need to naturally scale… like a BOSS!

Let's Make the Fifth Play

You are now ready to put your SCALE system in place.

Implement The Fifth Play, and then complete the checklist:

1. **S**OP's ____
2. **C**alendar System___
3. **A**utomation
   a. Lead Capture___
   b. Lead Conversion ___
   c. Client Onboarding ____
   d. Client Service Delivery & Updates ____
4. **L**ifetime Learning _____
5. **E**mail Campaigns
   a. Lead Magnet Delivery ____
   b. Short-Term Nurture ___
   c. Long-Term Nurture___

If you completed the checklist,
you have set up your scale foundation system

Congratulations!

Your Profit Pillar #5 -
Design a Scale System is in place.

Listen to my personal message and get a free 14-day trial of Keap, the CRM automation secret sauce tool behind my "work from wherever" life, by scanning the code on the next page with your smartphone or go to:

www.intellecttoincome.com/playfivekeap

Profit Playbook Finale

"Monetize You"

TIME TO BANK YOUR BRILLIANCE!

I've laid out the steps to achieving your lucrative lifestyle business, play-by-play, in this profit playbook. You now have the step-by-step plays for turning your intellect into income.

In **The First Play**, you learned that, before you start any business, you must set up your legal foundation. The best time to do that is at the onset, the next best time is now. You should never **SCIIP** this step. Start by making sure you have a proper *structure,* specifically a protective legal structure that will limit your liability so you will not be personally liable for the debts and liabilities of your business. Then, ensure you are using effective *contracts* to eliminate uncertainty, ensure consistent payment, and increase your business efficiency. Next, shield your *intellectual property* to protect your creative works and brand from copycats and thieves. You also want to get adequate *insurance* to shift your risk and protect against unanticipated business losses. Finally, you want to ensure you have *procedures and processes* in place, so your business runs efficiently and effectively, with and without your presence.

We then moved into **The Second Play**, assessing your intellect (degrees, education and experience) so you can become the attractive **EPPIC** expert character of your business. You will start by first identifying your area of *expertise* and putting your stake in the ground by professing your expert title to the world, just like Mohammed Ali did before he was the actual champion. Next, you will decide who you will serve, your *perfect dream client (PDC)*. Once you identify this person, the person who will most benefit from your area of expertise, you will then identify the one big urgent *problem* they need to solve *(UPS)*, that is in your expert genius zone. It is usually in the area of health, wealth, or relationships.

You will then create your *Instant Magnetizing Marketing Message (MMM)* so you can communicate to your PDC from the heart, like Safe Driver Towing, not from the head, as we saw with Babble Towing. You will then ensure you have *clarity* by creating your envision board to clearly identify where your PDC is (pain) and where they want to go (pleasure). Once you've completed the steps in The Second Play, you can move forward and build the bridge necessary to get your PDC from pain island to pleasure island.

In **The Third Play**, you learned how to build your offer solution bridge. Your solution bridge will provide **WINS** for both you and your PDC. Your proprietary Signature Offer System (SOS), your freedom framework, will be the bridge to provide those WINS. You will start building your solution bridge by *writing* out the step-by-step process (your signature framework) of taking your PDC from pain island to pleasure island.

Next, you will *identify* the objectives (pains, gains and content) of each step in your process. You will then give your framework a *name*. Lastly, you will then *select* the format by which you will deliver your solution (lead magnet, book, course, coaching, packages, etc.) The beautiful thing is your SOS bridge will allow you to meet your PDC where they are in their journey. If you are just connecting you can offer a lead magnet. If you are taking them up your offer value ladder (OVL staircase), you can offer them a different format of your solution. Once you have your signature offer system in place, you are ready to start enrolling your PDC into your services or programs and bringing them across the bridge.

In **The Fourth Play**, you learned how to enroll your PDC into your products, programs, and services. During the enrollment process, you must serve them the **MOST**. You start by getting into a service *mindset*. You are there to serve, not sell, and when you recognize this, the sale will come easily, they will likely enroll themselves. However, you must always be prepared to deal with *objections*. You should have a *script* but do not be scripted. The script is to help raise your PDC up as you guide them through the enrollment conversation until this becomes second nature to you. And most importantly, you want to *track* your numbers. What isn't measured is missed, and you don't want to miss hitting your profit goals.

In **The Fifth Play**, you learned the foundational **SCALE** method that you need to put in place at the onset of your business. Standard operating procedures (*SOPs*) allow you to have a written procedure for performing every key task in your business so when you are hiring and building a team, you won't have to waste time with redundant tasks or training new hires and re-training replacements. An automated *calendar* allows you to have a link ready 24/7 to give prospects without wasting time going back and forth trying to find a mutually convenient time to meet. *Automation* is critical to the client lifecycle. You have to be able to attract leads (target, attract, and collect leads with your lead magnets), convert (educate, offer, and close with your email nurture campaign) and create raving fans (deliver, offer more, and get referrals) automatically. This is a huge part of the scaling process. *Learning* is important. You have to commit to being a lifetime learner. Experts develop mastery, and they stay on top of their mastery by continuing to learn and elevate**.** Last, but not least, *email* growth is critical to scaling. You have to commit to growing your email list, so you have a list of potential buyers at your fingertips at all times. They say your income is in correlation to your email list. The rule of marketing says every email on your list represents $1 in monthly income. If you have an email of 1000, that email list is worth $1,000 monthly so if you want to grow your income, start by growing your list!

If you have completed all of your profit plays…

CONGRATULATIONS!

You are now ready to turn your intellect into income
and create a lucrative lifestyle business!

Do you need a more in-depth step-by-step implementation blueprint? Get *"Intellect to Income" – The Ultimate Profit Play Workbook:*

https://www.intellectotincome.com/workbook

What's Next?

If you are reading this page, that means you've completed *Intellect to Income: The Ultimate Profit Playbook,* and you're ready to implement your profit plays, or you've already done so along the way. With the insights gained from this book, you can transcend from commodity to attractive EPPIC expert and start monetizing YOU. Implementing the outlined plays will position you to leave that soul-sucking job behind, escape the time-draining career, and get off the entrepreneurial profit hamster wheel, so you can leverage your expertise and enjoy a lucrative lifestyle business.

If you have been inspired by this book and are ready to fully MONETIZE YOU, by implementing your profit plays and turning your wisdom into income, but you know you need additional accountability and support, don't worry, I'm not going to run off and leave you hanging. I would love to continue this journey side-by-side with you. Before I go, I want to offer you the opportunity to get the additional support you need.

If you would like to explore how I can help you implement your profit plays, turn your intellect into income, and build a lucrative lifestyle business, then I invite you to take the next step and complete the Intellect to Income Program Survey. It is confidential and only takes about 5 minutes to complete.

I have different program options because not all businesses and entrepreneurs are created equally.

https://www.intellecttoincome.com/survey

The survey will assess where you are and where you want to go so, I can determine which program will benefit you most.

Once your survey is submitted, I will personally review it. If it appears I can genuinely help you achieve your goals, my team will reach out to you to schedule a call. If that sounds good, complete the survey, and I look forward to speaking with you soon and, more importantly, providing you with the support, guidance, and accountability necessary to transform the way you are currently monetizing your intellect and scaling your business.

Cheers to your success along this journey!

Shevelle McPherson

Shevelle educates, empowers, and provides great value through her Intellect to Income programs. She goes above and beyond to ensure her clients' success. All her teachings, care, and support light a fire in you, providing hope and a full-proof system to grow your business and create the future you dream about. Thank you for making me love business again, believe in the future again, and feel alive!

—Cassandra Conway - Salon Owner & Hair Stylist
Founder of Natural Hair Care Extraordinaire, Philadelphia

Listen to my personal message and inquire about getting additional support in the Intellect to Income Program by scanning the code above with your smartphone or go to:

https://www.intellecttoincome.com/survey

About Shevelle

Shevelle McPherson, Esq. began her legal career as a prosecutor and an assistant district attorney for the City of Philadelphia. After several years of service, Shevelle set out on her entrepreneurial journey.

She formed McPherson Law and expanded her law firm to three locations in the first year. She is the founder and managing attorney of McPherson Law, a firm specializing in business and intellectual property, specifically trademark law. McPherson Law helps business owners own, protect, and monetize profitable brands with trademark protection.

As an attorney, Shevelle has received many accolades and recognition, including Top National Trial Lawyer; 10 Best Female Attorneys in Pennsylvania; Rising Star Super Lawyer, Pennsylvania; and Elite Intellectual Property Lawyer.

Shevelle is also the founder and CEO of Soar to Success Academy, an online coaching and consulting company that provides training for entrepreneurs and small business owners on how to get legally positioned for ultimate profit, protection, and peace of mind using her signature 5 Legal Pillar Profit System which she outlines in her legal playbook *Legally Bossed Up, The Ultimate Legal Playbook: How to Protect Your Business, Brand, and Profit So You Can Make More Money and Keep It.*

Through Soar2Success Academy, Shevelle provides training programs for high-achieving professional service providers, teaching them how to leverage and monetize their education, degrees, training, and experience by packaging it into a program, product, or service to create a lucrative lifestyle business.

Shevelle is extremely passionate about supporting entrepreneurs in launching, growing, and scaling businesses that are not only profitable but legally protected.

She is equally passionate about supporting professional service providers in creating an unshackled lifestyle businesses that provides time, location and financial freedom.

Connect with Shevelle

Websites:

McPherson Law: www.mcphersonlawoffices.com

Shevelle McPherson: www.shevellemcpherson.com

Online Academy: www.soar2successacademy.com

Legal Template Site: www.myprofitprotector.com

Email: info @shevellemcpherson.com

Get Legally Bossed Up VIP Membership:

www.legallybossedup.com/vipmembership

Get Legally Bossed Up- The Ultimate Legal Playbook:
www.legallybossedup.com/playbook

Get Legally Bossed Up – The Ultimate Legal Play Workbook
www.legallybossedup.com/workbook

Get Intellect to Income – The Ultimate Profit Play Workbook
www.intellecttoincome.com/workbook

Learn More About Shevelle – Get her Autobiography

www.legallybossedup.com/soar

Resources

Here is a list of the bonuses offered to assist you in implementing your profit plays!

BONUSES

1. Business Structure Comparison Chart
   https://www.intellecttoincome.com/bizchart

2. ITI Expert Factor Worksheet
   https://www.intellecttoincome.com/playtwoitifactor

3. SOS Brainstorming Worksheet
https://www.intellecttoincome.com/playthreesos

4. RAIISE Enrollment Script
https://www.intellecttoincome.com/playfourscript

5. CRM Access – Keap 14 Day Trial
www.intellecttoincome.com/playfivekeap

Made in the USA
Las Vegas, NV
03 November 2026

57423929R00067